Keep up the good Work, Charlie Brown!

by CHARLES M. SCHULZ

Selected Cartoons from
SPEAK SOFTLY, AND CARRY A BEAGLE, Vol. III

FAWCETT CREST • NEW YORK

KEEP UP THE GOOD WORK, CHARLIE BROWN

This book, prepared especially for Fawcett Crest Books, a unit of CBS Publications, the Consumer Publishing Division of CBS Inc., comprises a portion of SPEAK SOFTLY, AND CARRY A BEAGLE and is reprinted by arrangement with Holt, Rinehart and Winston, Inc.

Contents of Book: PEANUTS® comic strips by Charles M. Schulz
Copyright © 1975 by United Feature Syndicate, Inc.

ISBN: 0-449-23748-6

Printed in the United States of America

10   9   8   7   6   5   4   3   2   1

Keep up the good Work, Charlie Brown!

HERE COMES WOODSTOCK ON HIS NEW BICYCLE...
I HATE IT WHEN HE SAYS, "LOOK, NO WINGS!"
SCHULZ

Gentlemen,
I ordered a toy bicycle for my sister's doll set.
It was supposed to be here by Christmas. Perhaps it was delivered to the wrong address.
Would you look into the matter, please?
Thank you.
I REFUSE TO BE THE ONE WHO TELLS HIM!
SCHULZ

SNOOPY! WHY DON'T YOU COME INTO THE HOUSE, AND I'LL FEED YOU HERE? IT'S A LOT WARMER!
HOW NICE... AN INVITATION TO DINNER..
TAP
TAP
TAP
WHY DOES HE HAVE TO MAKE A BIG DEAL OUT OF EVERYTHING?
SCHULZ

STUPID DOG!

NEW YEAR'S WAS FIVE DAYS AGO, AND THAT DOG IS STILL CELEBRATING!

IT'S NEVER TOO EARLY TO CHECK YOUR MAILBOX FOR VALENTINES..
BUT FOR SAFETY'S SAKE, IT'S A GOOD IDEA TO STAND WAY BACK IN CASE A FLOOD OF VALENTINES COMES POURING OUT...
SIGH
SCHULZ